I Din't Say Nothin'!

Michael Brindid

Text © Nora Brindid 1999
Illustrations © Bridget Parsons 1998

First published 1995
This edition published 1999 by N Brindid
Orfanon
The Green
Hickling
Norwich
Norfolk NR12 0XR

Cover photograph courtesy
The Eastern Daily Press

ISBN 0 9525832 0 8

Also by Michael Brindid
I Dint' Say Nothin' Ag'in

In memory of Michael
1927 - 1998

Produced by Jim Baldwin
Fakenham, Norfolk

Printed in England

A Product of Fakenham

Foreword

Not since The Boy John letters were published in the *Eastern Daily Press* 36 years ago, have epistles in Norfolk dialect created so much interest.

Michael Brindid first wrote speculatively to the *EDP* in March '93 and since then his humour and perception in the Norfolk dialect have won him thousands of followers and established him as a Norfolk character. His regular letters have added an extra dimension to our very popular page and strike a chord with readers who love Norfolk and its heritage.

May I wish Michael and his book every success.

Peter Franzen
Editor
Eastern Daily Press

Introduction

There must be something in the Broadland air to inspire fresh backing for the true Norfolk chorus.

Just after the last war, Sidney Grapes started his much-loved correspondence to the *Eastern Daily Press*. The Boy John Letters were published in two volumes after his death in 1958 and became the cornerstone of the campaign to keep the local dialect alive.

Sidney Grapes lived all his life in Potter Heigham. Now, a few salt breezes away in the neighbouring community of Hickling, Michael Brindid has taken up the cudgel and the pen as that vital campaign continues towards the end of a century packed with grim forecasts about the imminent demise of our dear old vernacular.

The same unquenchable spirit is alive. The same dry humour is working its spell. The same objective to transform items of temporary amusement into a collection of permanent value must be applauded by all who care about the Norfolk way of life.

There are no rules when it comes to reproducing the sounds of broad Norfolk. You find a coat that fits as snugly as possible, and wear it proudly to defy the winds of change. Michael Brindid is "tannin' up his coller" against those who reckon it's high time Norfolk adopted a more fashionable wardrobe.

And he can practise what he preaches. I have seen and heard him in full cry at the annual dialect evening staged as part of the Cromer and North Norfolk Festival of Music and Drama.

He is not the new Boy John. He is the first Marster Michael. He is a worthy flagbearer as the fight goes on to underline Norfolk's differences – and to glory in them.

Keith Skipper
BBC Radio Norfolk

Acknowledgement

My wife has been the long suffering "Missus" throughout the writing of "I Din't Say Nothin'". Nevertheless she has been a tower of strength throughout, and it is to her I dedicate my book along with Norfolk people wherever they may be living. It is with gratitude that I say "Thank you" to Peter Franzen the Editor of the *Eastern Daily Press* for his foreword and his Staff for their encouragement.

Bridget Parsons, who also lives in the village of Hickling, was the ideal person to be asked to illustrate my letters. This she has done with care and dedication and I am very grateful to her.

Keith Skipper readily agreed to write the introduction. Through broadcasting and writing he has proved himself to be a true Norfolker and is doing all in his power to prevent the County from being manipulated and spoiled of its character.

Finally I must thank Jim Baldwin for getting this into print, something I thought would never happen! The vision has become a reality.

Michael Brindid
Hickling
March, 1995

She thought she'd got a cold comin' on.

Spinnin' a yarn

March, 1993

I're cum in my front room ter write this latter ter yew acorse my missus is in the back plearce boilin' sum onions fer har tea. She think she might a got a cold a-comin' on.

I say ter har, "Tha's wot yew git if yew sleep in a fild wi' the gairte open." She say, "Dorn't talk ser sorft."

My heart alive, Norridge City are a-doin' well ter year. I loike ter read about 'em in yar pearper on a Monda mornin'. I dorn't go now though I used to years ago an' never missed a gearme.

I went ter watch 'em one Sa'urda arternoon on my ole motor bike. My heart tha' wus suffen cold. When I cum humm, I say ter the missus, "I'm suffen cold." She say, "Tha's plenty good enough for yer, yew must be sorft goin' all tha' way in this wather ter watch grown up men kickin' a ball about."

She wus suffen savage. I say ter her, "Yer dorn't understand." Yer see she wanted ter go a-shoppin' an' I say ter her, "Tha's too cold fer tha'". She had a good ole go at me, but she wus orite when I told har I'd got sum chips in my pocket – she loike chips. Tha' put har in a good mind agin.

"I'm goin' ter set them agin'."

I Got Suffen Wrong off the Missus

April, 1993

My hart I got suffen wrong orf my missus larst Monda Mornin'. Tha's loike this here, she hen't hed a lot o' toime ter do har garden, so yisterda mornin' I see har go inter the ole shud, git har boike out, pump it up, an orf she go.

I shouted ter har, "Where are yew a- gorn'?" She say, "Out". "Rite," I thort, "Now's a good toime ter do har garden."

Well bor, I got stuck inter diggin' out all the ole lumber. There wus no ind on it. I thort, "She'll be suffen pleased."

When she cum humm about dinnertoime she say ter me, "Wot ha'e yew bin a-doin' on?" I say, "Your garden my luv." She say, "I'll cum an' hev a look." Tha's wen tha' all started. She shouted. I thought she wus a-gorn ter hev one o' har tanns. "Yu're dug up all my lillies" she say. "Don't talk ser sorft" I say, "Tha's ole bineweed." "Wot hev yer done wirrum?" she say. I say, "I hulled 'em up the ind o' the garden." She wus a bit orf fer the rest o' the dair. Enyhow I thort I'd tearke har ter Stallum Searle termorrer. She don't know yit.

Well we're bin an' we're back agin. We stayed the best part o' sum toime. I got har sum chips on the Searle ground an' a small half. Tha' put har in a good mind agin'. Then I see har go up the ole garden wirra pairl an' pick up all them ole bits o' lillies. She say, "I'm a-gorn ter set 'em agin. D'yer think they'll grow?" I say, "Yis" (but I dorn't think they will) I reckon cum next June toime I'll git wrong if they dorn't show through the ground.

She looked suffen happy.

Cen I cum an' watch?

April, 1993

I thort I'd let yer know I pleared my last gearme o' indoor bowls o' the season up there at Walsum tuther nite. My missus she say ter me: "Cen I cum an' watch?" I say: "Yis, tha'll be like ole times. We cen sit in the back o' the car an' hold hans." She say: "Dorn't talk ser soft, I aren't hev'n none o' that."

She got harself up a-rummin. She hed har new red skart on wot she got from the chapel jumble searle last Christmas, and a new pair o' them stockins wot cum up ter the wairst, and har high heeled shoes on, (the ones I got har fer our silver weddin). She looked suffin nice.

When I wus a'playin' I looked at har. She wus a-sittin' wir a bloke. They wur a-laughin' an goin' ahid. She had a packit o' crisps an' a small half. She looked suffen happy. I thort ter myself: "Thas a-rummin".

Arter the gearme, this blook, he went orf. I went over ter the missus. I say ter har: "Wus he up to?" She say: "Nothin".

"Wot hev you bina-talkin about?" I say. She say: "Nothin". She say: "He's lonely, he hent got a wife." "Blow that for a yarn," I thort.

Comin' home she wus in a funny good mind. She say ter me: "Are yer playin' next week?" I say: "No." She dint know tha' wus my larst gearme ter season, so tha'll put a stop ter har goin's on.

My missus go nowhere of a mornin' on har ole bike. Well she go nowhere nights an' all these days. I'm a-wonderin' if tha' bloke she met at Walsum ha' got enything to do wir' it.

The Parish Council were there well turned out.

The hul plearce look luvely rite now

June, 1993

The chairman o' our parish council hev arsked all on us wot live in the village ter trim up our plearces cors we're goin' ter see if we cen win the Best Kept Willage Competition wot your pearper run. We won it a few year ago an' I think we stand a good chance o' gittin' on it agin ter year corse the hul plearce look luvely rite now.

Tha' wus a big day for us when we won it afore. There wus people there from the council an' a blook from yar pearper takin' photos. The parish council were there well tand out. Our ole vicar, he was a-cuttin' about. He wus as pleased as a dorg wi' two tairls!

'As a pity them people wot cum round dornt cum an' look at my tairtas cus they look suffen good ter year. 'As a-corse I got sum new seed. My missus she say how about me sendin' you a pearper bagful o' nice new tairtas.

I say: "Dorn't talk sorft, if I do that then all o' them wot wark in his orfice ud want sum an' I hent go' enough fer that lot." I say ter har, wot abou' arskin' you over.

I cen teark you round our willage an' down ter the Broad. You cen call in fer a cup o' tea, then you cen teark a pearper bagful o' tairtas hum wen you go. Just let me know so I hev time ter put a clean shar' on.

Tha' wus suffen nice o' David Joyce (EDP, May 31) ter show concarn about my missus. I'm pleased ter say she hent bin a-goin' out nowhere on har ole bike ser much lairtly on account o' there a-bein' ser much wind (so she say).

I reckon she en'a seein' tha' blook now, do a little wind wunt stand in har way. I think she know where she's well orf, so per'aps tha's the ind on it, less hope so.

"Help me ter git down".

Tha was bewiful on one o' them EDP walks

July, 1993

Reckon you must be a-wonderin' wot a happened ter me as I hent writ ter you leartly. Me an' the missus a bin ter Spairn ter see our daugh'er an' har famly fer a few weeks. Tha's bi nice ter see 'em as we dornt go wery orfen an account o' tha' bein' ser hot.

The fust day back, we hetter git in the old garden. Tha' wus a job. We cut the grass an' hedges an' pulled the fat hin out o' the tearters, but tha's ship shearpe agin now.

When we wuk up tother mornin', my missus she say, "Tha's a luvly day, how about us goin' for a nice long walk?" I say, "Ha yer got anywhere in mind?" She say, "You git up an' go down an' bring me a cup o' tea up, an' I'll think o' suffen."

When I took har tea up she say, "We cen go on one o' them walks wot the EDP hev in their pearper." (She keep all o' them.) She found me one. Arter a time she got up, packed sum dinner an' orf we go.

We went ter Buxton an' walked acrors a gret ole field ter Oxnead. Tha' wus bewiful there near the river – swans, ducks an' all manner o' things. Then we wen' acrors a medda where there wus five hosses with their young uns. My missus thought they wa lovely. Arter a time we cum ter Brampton afore goin' back ter Buxton along the rearlway line.

Dorn't let on ter the missus I told yer this, but we ha'er climb over a five bar gearte. I got over alright, but when I looked back, there wus the missus on the top o' the gearte, one leg one side an' one leg tuther. She say, "Help me ter git down," so I go ter give har a hand an' she say, "Let me alone."

I larfed ter see har an' she got suffen savage. I say, "I reckon you'll hetter stay there all nite." She say, "Dorn't talk ser bloomin' sorft."

She go' down in the end. She dint hev too much ter say ter me arter tha' till we stopped an' hed our dinner an' a bit o' a rest.

When we were a-comin' home we passed a Fish an' Chip shop. The missus say, "Are they a- fryin'?" I say, "Yis." She say, "I'd like sum chips," so we got sum. We sat near the river an' et 'em. Tha' really wus a lovely day.

The missus she say, she hen't got nothin' ter say. She's busy a-stewin' rhubub. She reckon tha's good stuff – better than al yer tablets. She say, "Just look how tha' clean the ole saucepan out."

"Dad want the long weight."

There dornt seem ter be time, terday, fer them harmless pranks

August, 1993

I wonda how many times you hear yar starf say ter you, "I hent got time," or "I wish I hed more time." True there dorn't seem ter be ser much time on it these days.

When I fust star'ed wark in the buildin' treard, there seemed ter be more time fer a larf, a yarn an' a joke.

I remember goin' long o' my farther ter the harvest fild down at Master Alec Disney's ter mend a waggon tha' hed brook down. (Tha' ud be about a mile from the workshop.) We got ter this ole waggon, hulled sum sacks on the ground, an' Dad go' inter treard. I dint know wot he wus a doin' on.

I hant left schule wery long. He wus a usin' gret ole spanners, an' he soon go' covered in muck an' barley hans. I say ter him, "Wot cen I do?" He dint say nothin'. Arter a time I say, "Cen I help?" I spus he go' fed up wi' me arskin', so he say, "I want the long weight from the workshop, you ba''er go an' git it."

"Good," I thought, "Suffin' ter do at last," so I go' on my ole bike an' orf I go. When I opened the workshop door another carpenter was a-warkin' in there. He say, "Wha' do you want, boy?" I say, "Dad want the long weight."

He say, "Sit you down, I'll git it in a little while." Arter the best par' o' some time, I say ter him, "Hent I be''er be gittin' back?" He say, "I'll git it in a minute." I though' Dad ud be suffen savage. In the ind he say ter me, "You be''er git back now, you've had a long enough wait."

A few years on I wus a-warkin' on a site at Catfield right near the rood. Afore we left orf, we ha''er put red lights near the buildin'. The foreman sent a boy ter git sum paraffin. He cum back wi' Esso Blue. The foreman meard him go all the way back, sayin' tha' wus no good, they wanted Pink Paraffin fer red lights.

How many boys were sent ter the ironmongers ter git straight hooks or wire nettin' seed! Terday there dornt seem ter be time fer them harmless pranks.

I can't mearke ens ner middles out o' my missus o' learte.

We hed chops fer dinner yisterdee, then she give me my sweet. I say ter har, "Wha's this?" She say, "Banana custed." I say, "Where's the banana?" She say, "I dint hev one." She hent bin harself since her linen line brook.

Back ter the coach a-puffin an' blowin.

One o' them there mystery tours

September, 1993

My missus a bin suffen busy just leartly so I say to har, "There's a coach gorn on one o' them there mystery tours, shall we go?" She says, "Yis", so I booked sum seats.

We left about nine. Nobody knew where we war a-goin', only the driver, an' he warn't sure. Arter a nice ride we ended up in Lavenham for dinner. There wus time ter hev a good ole jam about afore we hed our meal. Tha's a funny ole pleace. The buildin's are all on the skew. If one on 'em were ter fall down, the hul lot ud go.

Arter dinner we went an' had a look round the Church. Tha' wus bew'iful. Me an' my ole mearte Tom stood an' looked at them lovely stearned glass winders for everser long. Tom reckoned tha' they're the best winders he'd ever sin.

The day we war there, they were a-puttin' yaller lines on the road. Tom's missus stepped orf the pearvement an' put har foot in the wet pearnt an' go' it all on har shoe. She mobbed. She say ter the blook tha' wus a-doin' on it, "You should hev some nootices up." He say, "I can tell where you lot come from." My hart she looked at him. He din't say no more.

I must tell yer this. My missus, she's the master one out fera-losin' umbrellas, so she dint tearke one with her corsa she dint hev one, so she took har red mac instead. As we ware agittin' on the coach, she say ter me, "Where's my mac?" I say, "I dorn't know." she say, "I must a left it where we hed our dinner, go an' git for me." I say, "You left it there, you go." She warn't wery pleased. She go' back ter the coach a-puffin' an' a-blowin'. She was suffen savage.

Orf we go agin'. We went over tha' gret ole river bridge near Ipswich. Tha's a good bit o' wark tha' is. My missus wus suffen glad when we go' over th'other side.

We finished up at Felixstowe. Me an' the missus walked in the gardens. I say ter har, "Can you remember us a-comin' here when we ware a-courtin'?" She say, "I try not to."

Arter a nice tea, we mearde our way hoom. On the way we saw a sign on the side o' the rood tha' said, "Free Church". My missus say, "We ba''er go there, tha'll be cheaper than our Mathodist." I say, "Tha' dorn't mean tha'. When you see a sign wot say Free House tha' dorn't mean you cen git a small half fer nothin'." She say, "I dint look at it like tha'."

You can see for miles up there

A good toime was 'ad at the garden par'y

September, 1993

You can say wot you loike, we dorn't git the nice summer dairs an' evenins loike we used ter git. I wus a-talkin' ter the missus abou' it. She say she dorn't think we'll git really nice wather agin till we git a chenge o' governmen'.

She say: "We go' boo'iful wather when we had Lairber in." I say: "Tha's go' nothin' ter do wirit." "Orite Knowall," she say, "Cen you tell me where all the wa'er a gone out o' our Chapel pit, tha' wus allus full til the Tories took uver?" Or, she say: "Tha' could be suffen ter do wi' them ole nuclear power stairtions."

Howsumever, tha' held fine a' our garden par'y for the chapel. My har' there wus sum lo' o' people cum. They maird over £500 pound. We're bin a'goin ter the sairme garden orf an' on fer years now. There's a tall ole mill there tha' go wi' the house where people cen go up an' walk around. You cen see fer miles up there.

A holida mairker cum down an' told one o' the locals tha' he could see the ships a-cumin' out o' Amsterdam harbour. "Straight out there" an' he pointed in tha' direction. This local reckon he wus sorft, he wus a-poin'in ter one o' them ole oil rigs orf Bacton. We all had a good ole larf abou' it.

There wus all sorts o' bowlin' gairmes wi' sum good prizes. A woman hed a go on one. Har fust ball missed the board altergather. The blook tha' wus in charge say ter har: "You can't hit a barn door." (Just larfin'.) She wus sum put out an' stumped orf. She din't bother ter hull no more o' her balls.

My missus wus on the jumble. They dun very well. Arterwards she say ter me: "We mairds over £80 an' there wus just as much stuff left uver as wot we hed ter star' with. I carn' mairke tha' out cen you?"

We had two hosses, one white an' one black an' they hed ribbons on their tairls – they looked suffen nice. Two gals were a-runnin' up an' down all arternume tairkin' kids fer rides. I bet their legs airked b'the time they'd done (the gals' I mairn).

The woman wot opened it (she warn't a Norfolk woman, bu' she done har best an' spook wery well), she said she hoped we'd all hev a good toime an' we did.

My hart tha' wus a job.

Trouble with the chimly

October, 1993

Tha's a bloomin' good job you din't cum round and see me an' the missus the nite afor last, corse we had a rite ole carry-on here.

Wot wi' one thing an' another, we din't git round ter sweepin' the chimly in the spring, so the missus say ter me: We'll ha''er git tha' done afor we start fires agin, corse tha's gitten a bit nippy of a nite now.''

She say: "I'll book the sweep." I say: "How much dew he corst?" She say: "Over a fiver." I say: "I'll do tha' fer a lot less than tha'." She say: "Cen you dew it?"

I say: "Dorn't tork sorft, corse I cen dew it?" So I wen' round an' saw my nearbour Stan ter see if I could borrer his rods an' brush. (He'a got all tha' sort o' gear.) "Corse yer cen," he say, so arter tea I hed a go.

The missus took the pictures down an' covered the clock wirra bi' o' newspearper. I say: "Dorn't you dew na more, I shan't mearke ner mess." I go' a duss sheet out o' the shed, put it over the man'elpearse an' held i' on wi' two gret ole stuns. Everything wus ready, so orf I go.

I soon go' the hang on it. The missus say: "I dorn't know why you hen't dun this afor." I say: "You batter git a torch an' go out an' tell me wen the brush cum out o' the top." Arter a bit she cum in, she was suffen pleased, she say: "Yer dun it."

I took the rods down. I say: "Where's the brush?" She say: "I dorn't know." Then she started. "I should a go' a proper man ter dew it." I dussn't tell yer wot she called me. She din't harf git har sha' out.

I ha''er git a ladder, climb up the ole roof an' stand on the ridge ter look inter the pot an' there wus the brush on one rod abou' four foot down. I go' a hoe ter try an' fish i' up agin. I go' i' in the ind, but my hart, tha' wus a job.

So wen you do call round an' see me, wotever yer do, dorn't say nothin' about sweepin' chimlees corse tha's a sore point. I'm hopin' the missus'll cum round arter a bit, but I dorn't think she'll be askin' me ter sweep the front room. (Tha' wus the livin' room I done.)

"My teeth! git the tongs."

The Missus is gittin' wery Fergitful O' Learte

November, 1993

We hent hed a holida fer a few year now since our mawther Carol moved ter Spairn. We go an' see har instead, but tha' ent wot I call a real holida. Wot wi' the missus a-washin', cookin' an' helpin' ter look arter the granchildren, tha' fair ter tearke it out on us. We aren't as young as we wa five year ago.

The missus say ter me, "We or'er hev a few dairs away somewhere. A long week-end." I say, "Orite, we could go on our Weddin' Anniwassary." She say, "Tha's uver enit? I thought tha' wus in June." I say, "Why din't yer say suffen then?" She say, "I fergo'" "How mana year hev we bin married?" I say. She say, "Too long, tha's toime I trearded yew in fer a younger model." I say, "Tha's stupid a-torkin' loike tha'".

The missus is gittin' wery fergitful o' learte. Tha's har bathdair afore long. She're bin the searme airge now fer manna year, she'r fergot how old she realla is. I think I're go' a good idea. She wus born just afore or just arter the war, but I can't ramamber which it is.

She dun a job tuther nite. She'd bin ter the dentist ter hev a couple o' teeth out. He mearde har a new plearte an' say, "They might hart a bit ter statt with, if so tearke 'em out occairsionlla." Sunda nite she wus a-eatin' an oringe an' warn't half enjoyin' it. She put all the pill on a plearte, then when she finished she hulled it on the fire, teeth an' all. She say, "Michael" (she dorn't orfen call me tha') "My teeth, I hulled 'em on the fire, git the tongs."

Corse yew know wot happened to 'em. She wus sum upset. She he''er go back ter har dentist. She sat ter him, "Yew'll niver believe wot I're done ...." He say he hed a woman whose dorg et hars. Another passon flushed theirs down the loo. I think tha' mearce har feel a bit ba''er but tha' din't alter the fact th' she ha''er pay all uver agin, or rather I hed to.

That'll learn ya to think what you're doing a bit more.

My missus a got a new bike

December, 1993

The larst time I rit ter you, I meant ter tell yer my missus a got a new bike. Wen I say "new", 'as nearla new. She got it orf har sister who reckon tha' wen' tew farst, so the missus bort it orf on a. Tha's alrite but tha' hent got lites on it. I say "Tha's a good job, praps tha'll keep you in of a nite." She larft, she knew wha I meant.

Wot I realla wont ter tell yer is this – Sum time ago, she wen on her bike (not har new one, she dint hev tha' then) ter a concer' at our willage schule. Arterwards she go' a-torkin' ter sum o' the mums an walked hum wirum. Wen she went ter git har bike out o' the shud a few dairs learter, tha' warn' there. She say ter me, "Hev you had my bike?" I say, "No". She say, "Well tha' ent in the shud". She looked in the other little shud, (tha' wus the other plearce years ago afor we wen on the sewer) an' tha' warnt there. She say, "Do you think someone a pinched it?" She wus suffen put out at not hevin' har ole bike, corse you know wot she's like fer a-goin' out nowhere on it.

Arter sum time she wus tellin' the schule caretearker how she'd lorst har bike, an' this woman told har tha' the Hidmarster hed kept it fer a week mairkin inquiries with no results so he rang the Police Steartion an' a policeman had bin an' fetched it. Blow me if I din't hatter go up ter Stalham Police Steartion an' git it. I say, "Praps tha'll larn yer ter think wot yer a-doin' a bit more." I wus suffen savage.

Now shea got tew bikes she say ter me, "You can hev my old un. I know tha' ant a lo' o' good." But warnt tha' nice o' har ter think o' tha! She can be everser kind, but not wery orfen – jus' now an' agin'.

You never saw such a job.

Hope you all hev a nice Chrismas

December, 1993

My missus a mearde har Chrismas puddins. She allus mearke har own – hev done eversince we got married.

She hev two or tree in the bottom o' har coppa an' sum more on the stuv. She hev the winders an' doors open ter let out the steam. There's water runnin' down the walls – you niver saw such a job. She mixed up all the stuff the day afore. She go' sum stout an' put in 'em (she reckon tha' give 'em a nice dark colour). She hed a can o' stout ter spare so she say, "You cen hev tha' arter tea".

Arter tea I thought "I'll hev tha' tin o' stout" so I went ter the pantry, I say "Wha' hev yer done wi' my stout?" She say, "I hed it".

She reckon she's a-goin' ter do har cearke next. I say, "Why dorn't yergit one out o' the shop?" She say, "Yer dorn't know wus in 'em." She mearke a lot o' soursage rolls an' mince pies corse the dustmen an' pusman like one wi' their corfee. There's one o' them pusmen seem ter stay a long time (so I'm told) I can't mearke tha' out.

This is a good time ter thank all o' them people wot rite ter me a-tellin' me how much they like my latters. I hed a good larf tuther mornin'. A blook asked me fer my autograph. How about tha'! Then a woman tell me how she send my latters ter someone in New Zealand who used ter live in Norfolk an' moved out there ter live. Tha's a-rummon all tha' way away.

I'd like to wish you an' your Staff a Happy Christmas an' a peaceful New Year, I'll write agin wen I git harf a chance. My missus she say she hope you all hev a nice Christmas. (She seem ter be in a very good mind at the moment).

He Say: "Whats in there?"
I Say: "Plum puddings."

Well, me an' the missus a bin ter Spain

February, 1994

I reckon you're a-wonderin' where I're bin a-gettin' to corse I hent writ ter yer fer the best part o' sum toime. Well me an' the missus a bin ter Spain ter see our mawther Carol fer nigh on a month.

Tha' wus suffen nice ter see har an' har family as we dorn't see 'em wery orfen. Tha' wus luvely wather all the toime we were there. When we were at the airport we began ter think we were never goin' ter git there. Tha' wus the missus fault. I told har not ter use foil puddin' bearsins, but you know wot she's loike, you can't tell har nothin', she think she know the lot.

Anyhow, we got rid of our cearses orite. Then we went ter this here Customs plearce. We put our hand luggage an' the missus blue coat on tha' movin' tearble. Wen we went round tuther side, a blook say ter me, "Is this your bag?" I say, "Yis." He say "What's in there?" I say, "Plum puddins". He say, "If they're plum puddings my name is John Major," so the missus say, (just larfin' like) "Mornin' Mr Major."

My hart he looked at har. I thought he wus goin' ter git his sha' out but he dint. He hed a good look in an' tha' wus orite. Then a woman wot stood near ter him say ter the missus, "There's something showing up in your handbag, may I have a look?" The missus say, "Do wot yer loike", so she tipped all the stuff on the tearble, you never saw ser much on it, an' blow me if she dint hev a knife in there wot she use for a-pillin' apples. Wen the missus told har wot she use it for, this woman say, "That's fine, have a Happy Christmas."

Lairter on, I got on ter har about the plum puddins.

She say, "I wunt a mearde the blomin' things if I could a told." She reckon she thort the woman wus nice but she dint go nothin' on the blook, she thort he wus sorft ... She say, "Wot about wen we git ter Madrid, how a' we goin' ter explairn ter tha' Spanish lot wot a plum puddin' is?", but we got through orite an' our Carol wus there wi' har two li''le gals ter meet us.

The missus bin feelin' a bit under the wather

February, 1994

My hart tha's bin a job abow' here this larst day o' two as the missus, she're bin feelin' a bit under the wather. She wen ter bed tuther night an' reckon she felt a bit weak. I larft, I say, "Tha's ba''er than feelin' a for'night." She din't think tha' wus wery funny.

Enyhow, cum the mornin' she got up just arter seven. Soon as ever har feet hit the boards, she reckon the room went round an' round. I say, "You ba'er cum back inter bed afor you blunder down the stairs." I got up an' went down an' mearde her a cup o' tea.

Wen I took it to har, blow me if she warn't asleep, so I din't wearke har up. Arter abou' harf an hour she shouted, "Michael" (she dorn't orfen call me tha'). I say, "Yis my luv." "Wen are you a-goin' ter bring me a cup o' tea?" "In a minute" I say.

I go' on wi' the housewark – I washed the plairts an' done the stove riddy ter lite a fire. There was the missus a- shoutin' agin, "Hev you bin an' got the pearper yit?" I say, "No." "Well tha's time you hed" she say.

I din't say nothin' abou' tha' other cup I'd took her. She had har cup o' tea an' tha' seemed ter cheer har up a rummin'.

Wen I took it to har she say, "Din't you bring my glasses?" Tha's how tha' wus all the mornin', "Do this an' do tha'", I wus suffen glad wen she went orf ter sleep agin' just so I could hev a bit of a rest. I went inter the backplearce an' put the wireless on low so I din't wearke har up. She din't want a lot o' dinner so I lit the fire an' she cum down abou' half arter two. She said she felt a lot ba''cr.

I mearde a beef stew wi' carrots, onions an' tearters. (I put an Oxo in) I thort tha' ud do har good. Granfar John, he used ter say, "If yer dorn't feel up ter a lot you want ter walk sum grub into yer."

My stew did the missus a lot o' good. She watched Emmerdairle Farm, then went back ter bed, leavin' all the washin'-up fer me to do.

In the mornin' she wus back ter har ole self agin', so wotever she hed din't last long I'm pleased ter say. I dorn't want a day like tha' agin' in a hurra.

I thor' she'd be orite cum Tharsday corse tha's the day she go nowhere on har ole bike.

"On the ole phone a-larfin' an' goin' ahid."

She even brort me a cup o' tea in bed ...

March, 1994

Ire hed a problem just leartle, in fact tha's bin a bit worryin'. Tha' all statted on Valentine's Daire. The pust cum an' there was one fer the missus. She opened it up an' put it in har pocket so I shunt see it. I say, "Who's it from?"

She din't say nothin'.

I didn't think enymore abou' it, but from then on, she 'a bin suffen' happy. I carn't mearke it out, nothin' is too much trouble. She 'er go' a smile on har fearce an' she call me luvely nairmes. Tha' must be tree weeks ago now an' she's still the sairme.

She go abou' the house a-singin' an' she even brort me a cup o' tea in bed tuther mornin' an' cleaned my best shoes. She dorn't even arsk me ter do the washin' up no more. I keep tryin' ter think wus brort this on, but I'm blowed if I know wus up wirrer. Mind you, I arn't cumplairnin' cors I're niver bin looked arter ser well afore. Anyway, at larst I think I're go' ter the bottom on it.

The missus say. "The Librer van cum terdaire hev you go' any books ter go back?" I say, "Yis, I'll git 'em fire yer." She say, "There's a book next ter the bed, gor'n git it luv", so I picked up this here book an' noticed a card a-stickin' out on it.

I pulled it out an' blow me if tha' warnt a Valentine's card. I thor' ter myself, "She's up ter har ole tricks." I put the card back in the book 'an giv it to har an' din't say nothin'.

I cum in tuther mornin' an' hard har on the old phone a-larfin' an' goin' ahid. I went out agin so she didn't know I'd hard har. Now Mr Editor, do I say suffin' ter har abou' it, or do I keep quiet? If I say suffin' tha' might put a stop ter this good life I'm enjoyin', an I dorn't want tha' ter happen.

Wot would you do? Do yer think I orta write ter one o' them there women's books ter them people wot arnswer latters, or leave things as they are an' let it sort itself out? No matter how yer look at it, tha's a rum ole' job don't yer think.

Sold to:- "The woman in the blue coat".

Yew wanta keep yer Hans in yer Pockets

March, 1994

The Missus dun har washin' on Monda Mornin'. She allus hev done ever since we're bin married. She went in the ole shud ter git har pegs an' she say ter me, "The back tyre on my bike is flat, I ba''er pump it up ter see if tha' hold." She hung out har linen an' went in the shud. She say, "My tyre is flat agin, I reckon I must agot a puncture. Cen yew mend it for me corse I wan' ter go out on it termorrer mornin'?"

I say, "Where are yew a-gorn' shiggin' orf to?" She say, "Niver yew mind."

"Enyhow," I say, "I hent got the gear," She say, "Yew did hev, I'll go an' see if I cen find it." So she went in the shud agin'. Arter sum toime she cum in wirra big ole biscuit tin. "Tha's all in this here tin" she say. "I thort yew hed sum. Yew can't git out on it now." I say, "I hen't got my levers." She say, "My farther used ter use fork handles." She found me two o' har old ones, (Not har best ones) so I thort I ba''er do it for har corse she ent a bad ole sort really.

Cum the mornin' she wus up loike a shot. She say, "Tha's a nice mornin' I think I'll go out." So she got harself up an' orf she go. I thort ter myself, "I wonder where she's a-gorn."

She cum back abou' tree. She say, "I're hed a rum ole mornin'. I went on Stallum Searle Ground jus' ter hev a look. The arctioner wus a-sellin' a lot o' ole lumber, so I stopped a minute." She reckon a friend o' hars wot stood over the other side wairved ter har. She say, "I wairved back an' the orctioneer say, 'The woman in the blue coat'. I wus movin' away ter spearke ter my friend, wen one o' the helpers cum up ter me, Gev me a ticket an' say, "Yew cen pay now or in the office." The missus say, "I dorn't know wot yew mean." This blook say, "Y're just bort a roll o' wire nettin'." She say, "Tha' I hen't." He say, "Yew put yer hand up an' he took yer bid." "Wudder I want wi' a roll o' wire nettin'?" she say. He told her ter keep sum hins. She told him she din't want ner hins, an' how much wus it. He say, "£4.50." She say, "My ole man unt be wery preased if I go hum wi' a roll o' wire nettin'. Enyhow, how em I gorn ter git tha' hum on my bike?" Somebody pointed out the blook tha' wus also a-biddin' an' he took it orf har hans. She recon she wus suffen pleased.

I say ter har, "Next toime yew go there yew wanta keep yar hans in yer pockets," She larft.

The steam 'll mearke the ink run.

Me an' the Missus at the Cromer Festival

March, 1994

Me an' the Missus hed a good time tuther nite. We went ter the Cromer Festival ter tha' there Norfolk Dialec' Readin' do. I took part. I allus thort I'd like ter hev a go. Well bor, there wus some mess o' people there. Wen they called out yer nearme yew hatter go up on the stearge an' read fer two or tree minutes. I thort I wus gorn ter hev a tan wen I saw all them people a-gorpin' at me, but I kept a-gorn' an' got tru it orite. Arter I'd done, I got a clap an' tha' mearde me fair a lot batter. Then we hatter hang about a while time the judge sorted out his thoughts an' mearde his noots. In the ind they called me out ter go an' git a sustificut. I felt as proud as a dorg wi' two tearls. My missus say, "Do yer think yew'll be on Television?" I say, "Dorn't tork ser sorft." She say, "Everabody hatter start somewhere. Barnard, (or rather Sar Barnard) Matthews, he statted orf wi' a few ole hins in his back yard, an' tearke R.G. Carter, he statted orf in a small way an' look where ther'e got to now." I say, "Tha' en't the searme sort o' thing."

Cum the mornin' I put sustificut on the pantra door. I thort people 'ud see it there corse tha's rite in front on 'em when they cum ter my back door. My Missus say, "Tha's no good hevin' tha' there, corse the steam from the copper 'll mearke the ink run. You know wot tha's like in here of a Monda mornin'." So I took it down agin an' purrit on the mantlepearce in the front room. I thort tha' looked nice there, but hang you on, wen the missus cum she say, "Tha's stupid puttin' on it there, you know the ole chimmly smoke wen the wind is in the East, tha'll soon git covered in soots." I say, "Tha's a rummin' tha' is, I go trew all tha', I git a sustificut, now I can't find nowhere ter put it. Wot em I gorn ter do wirrut?" She say, "I could tell yet but yew wunt like it." So I put it back in the envelope an' hulled it on top o' the wardrobe an' tha's where tha' is now.

The fact is, she dorn't want it nowhere. I think she's a bit jealous, you know wot she's like.

You niver see ser many kippers.

I say ter the missus, I'll tearke yer fer a ride

April, 1994

Tha's bin suffen quiet about here of an evenin' over Easter corse the missus a bin shiggin' orf a-singin' wi' them there Hawkeswood Singers.

There's just over tharty on 'em. They all dress the searme. They hev black skats (the women I mearne) an' white shats an' red ganzies. As well as lookin' well tanned out, they mearke a nice noise. The missus enjoy singin' along wirrum, tha' git har out o' the house, an' tha's nice fer me ter be on my own sometimes corse you know wot she's like.

Cum Easter Munda tha' wus a-rairnin' and' a-blowin' an carryin on, an' tha' wus enuff ter flair yer. I say ter the missus, "Hev yer got ter go out ternite?" She say, "No." I say, "Less hev an arly dinna an' I'll tearke yer fer a ride." She say, "Tha'll be nice Michael," I knew ba the look on er tha' plearsed er. So arter dinna she say: "Do I wonta dress up?" I say: "Yis." So she put on har black dress, har black cut (not har blue one) an' har high-heeled shoes. She put a dab o' this an' tha' on har fearce. She looked a treart – I'd fergot she could look ser nice. Anyway, orf we go. She wus suffen excited. She say: "Where-a we a-gorn, is it sumwhere nice?" I say: "You weart an' see."

We wen' thro' Cromer an' Sherinum on ter Cley. I stopped in the willage an' went ter the Smuk House where they mearke them luvely kippers. The woman wot own the shop shew me round. I had a look in the smuk-house. Well bor, you niver see ser many kippers. She was a-tellin' me herrin' they use cum from Norway. They hed salmon in there an' all. I say ter har: "How's the best way ter cook a kipper?" She say: "You wanta git hold on it by the tearle an' drop it in a jug o' boilin' water fer a few minutes, that's all yer gotta do," I dorn't know if many o' your readers know that, but she reckon the're bewaful done like tha'.

We got back ter the car an' the missus say: "Where-a we agorn to now?"

I say: "Home." My hart she kicked up a dulla. She say, "Do yer mearne ter tell me I're got myself all up just ter cum an' look round a smuk-house an' ter buy a pair o' kippers? Is tha' yar idea o' romance?" She din't say nothin' ter me a-comin' home till we got ter Salthouse. I stopped the car. She say: "Wher a yer goin' to now?" I went acrorse the rood ter git a crab an' cum back an' giv it ter har. I say: "Here yar my luv, you can't say I dorn't luv yer now." She cearme round arter a bit.

"I've fergot ter tan the oven on."

Tha' ole chicken is still cold, she say

April, 1994

Hev yer got ter the stearte where you fergit things? If you hev Mr Editor, then you'll know wat I'm on about. Like in yar orfice, I bet you say sumtoimes, "Where's tha' latter I hed a minute ago? Where's my pen?" or, "Hev enyone sin my car-keys?"

Tearke my missus, tha' wus Motherin' Sunda so she say "We'll hev a chicken fer our dinner." She got everything riddy, put it in the ole oven wi' sum beaked teartus, then set the toimer. She say, "Tha's all riddy. All I're gotter do is ter mearke the batter puddin' when I git home an' we'll hev a nice dinna."

So me an' the missis went up ter the Motherin' Day Sarvice. There's sum lot o' people tan out fer tha'. They give all the mothers a little bunch o' flowers. They all loike tha' corse tha' mearke 'em feel suffen special – an' so they are.

Enyhow, we git home, lookin' forward ter our dinna. The missus go inter the back plearce ter put har batter puddin' in. She cum inter the front room ter me. "I're dun a job, I're fergot ter tan the oven on" she say, "Tha' ole chicken is as cold now as it wus wen I put it in." She say, "We'll hev it fer tea instead." I say, "No my luv, bein's as Mother's Daire I'll tearke you out ter dinna." I hed giv har a bar o' chocklet an' a packet o' crisps ter mark the occairsion, but I thort hevin' someone cook dinna fer har would be nice.

"Well wa's wrong wi' tha'?" I hear you say. Hav you ever tried ter git a dinna on Motherin' Sunda wirrout a-bookin' fust. Well bor, we went all over the plearce. Tha' wus a job. In the ind we got in at a plearce at East Russen an' hed a nive meal. Arter dinna we had a look round Russen corse tha's wher the missus lived afor I married har, an' tha's where we did our courtin', but tha's enuff o' tha'.

Talkin' about fergittin', another thort a now cum ter me, my farther, he wus a carpenter afor me. He wus tellin me about a blook he warked with who mearde a shud an' boarded it up all the way round an' fargot ter leave a doorway, so tearke heart Mr Editor, wen you do start ter fergit things, just remember tha' happen ter all on us at sum toime or other.

Where the flyin' ha you bin?

Suffin' busy but I thort I're got orf lite!

May, 1994

Wot wi' one thing an' another, the missus a bin suffin' busy. She hent hed time to do har spring cleanin'. So she say: "I think I'll just give it the once uver ter year." I thort ter myself: "As a bloomin' good job, I hairt spring cleanin' time." Tha' allas tearke two a tree months ter know where enything is arter she'r done.

She say, "One thing we'd batter do's the lite sheards. We'll hatter tearke 'em down an' brush the cobwebs orf on 'em." I looked at 'em an' I say: "I see wot yer mean." She say: "We hen't got eny steps now. You brook 'em if you rememba." I say: "So I did."

She say: "That nice man thata moved inta the new house up the road a got some coarse I're sin 'em. I'll gorn see 'im. He'll let me hev'em for a harf an hour." I dorn't know 'im, but the missus say he's werry nice. He live all on his own. Sum people say he hent got a wife so I say: "I'll gorn see 'im." She say: "No, 'as orite, I'll go."

She was gone the best part o' sometime. When she got back I say: "Where the flyin' ha you bin?" She say: "He wanted ter show me round his house." I say: "He must a got a grat ole' house. You could a looked round Blicklin' Hall in tha' time." She didn't say nothin'.

We took all the sheards down. She cleaned 'em an' I put 'em back. There wern't anuff room fer the steps on the pantry floor, so I say: "We'll learve that one, no one'll see in there."

"We're gorn ter do it" she say, "Coarse tha's daty." She got a tall ole' stool. "This'll dew it," she say. I say: "I arn't gorn on them." She say, "Cum out o' the way you sorft ole' fool, I'll dew it." So she got on the top o' this stool. She say: "You batter hold me – not like that!" she say (she larft).

I thort if tha's all the spring cleanin' she's gorn ter do ter year I're got orf lite. I say: "I'll tearke the steps back." "Tha's orite," she say, "I'll go." As she was a cumin' out o' the pantry she say: "I really must put some clean pearpa on the shelves." She looked on one shelf, tha' said "May 1987." She say: "Tha's bin her seven years. Tha's time tha' cum orf."

She allas use the EDP fer har shelves, she say tha' cover more ground than them ole' London pearpa's. She cut a nice pattern on the front wi' a pair o' sissors, then fold it down wi' drawin' pins.

Arter she'd down she say ter me, "Tha' look batter dorn't it?" I say: "Yis my luv."

So he took the pleart an all.

The missus meard the fust row too long

May, 1994

I're got suffin' rong agin. Tha's a pity corse werrabin a gittin' on werry well just learly.

The missus say: "Would yer like me ter help yer in the garden?" I say: "Yis my luv, you can set sum seeds." She had a packet o' carrots an' beart.

She say: "Tha' say on the packet 'Sow in rows a foot apart' but that' dornt tell her how long the rows agot ter be." So she meard a drill, an' set a row. Then she meard another one an' set sum morem, but they onla went harf way acrorse. "See wot I mearne," she say. I say ter har: "You meard the fust row too long." "How can yer tell how far the're gorn to go?" she say.

She kept on an' on abow' it. In the ind she say: I're had anuff onit, Um gorn in agin."

Arter a while I looked in the winda. There she wus, feet up, readin' the pearper wirra cup o' corfee. I say ter har: "Arn't yer gorn ter do ner more?" She say: "No, I'll do the dinner." So I went up the ole' garden agin. If yer want ter know the truth onit, I gont on a lot batter on my own!

About one or a little arter, she give me a shout ter cum sum wittles. I say ter har: "What hev yer got?" She say: "A bit o' pork, will yer carve it?" Tha' was a nice big bit. I cut orf the rind, she say: "I'll put tha' on a little plearte, tha'll do fer the bads."

So she put it out on the lorn.

Arta we had our dinner we both onus had four'y winks. The missus cum round fust. She hallered at me. She say: "There's a grat ole dorg on the lorn a gittin' tha' meart I put out fer the bads. Gorn git rid onit."

Wen I opened the front door that' ole' dorg hard me a cummin'. He grabbed the rind, tha' wus stuck ter the pleart, so he took the pleart anall. He ran acrors the garden an' onta the road. The pleart dropped orf an' brook. I picked up the bits 'o pleart an' give 'em ter the missus. Well bor din't she carry on. Her fearce went red. She say: "If yer hent a gone arter tha' ole' dorg, tha' wont a happened. Tha's al yar forit, you'll soon crearse me. Tha's on a my willa pattern plearts wot cum from Aunt Mollie."

I din' say nothin', tha's best not to wen she's in tha' sort o'mind.

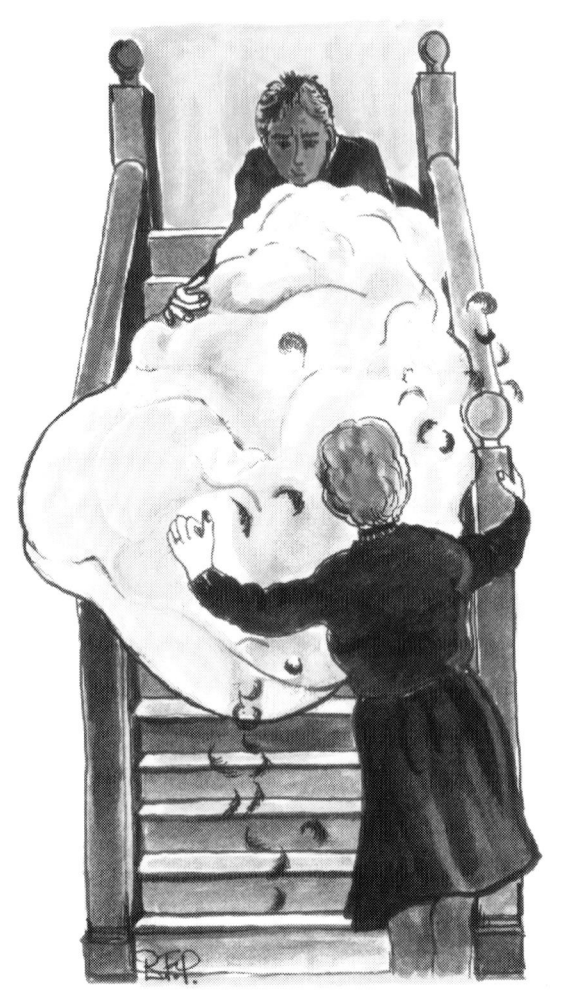

"You give the ole thing a push."

There wus faathas evrawhere

June, 1994

Our Mawther Carol is back home wirrus, wi' har two kids fer a few weeks, an' she took' em ter the beach at Pallin'. Comin' home, blow me if she din't hev a bit of an accident. No one wus haat, tha's the mearne thing. Lucky fer me my 'ole mearte Pete tha' keep the garage just acrors the rud, he's a-gorn ter doit for me. He say: I'll soon git tha' ship shearp agin.''

So the missus say: "Tha's no good, we'll hatter go ter Stalum ter do sum shoppin', we'll go on our 'ole grids". I say: "Tha's tree mile, I dorn't fell like a-bikin' all tha' blinkin' way." She say: "Tha'll do yer good." She hed har new bike an' I hed har old un. Tha' wus nice really. I say: "Tha's like 'ole times wen we werra cortin', but tha's a long time ago." She say: "Yis, an' I fare ter bin gorn uphill an' hid wind ever since." I say: "I wish you wun't say things like tha'."

I carn't mearke har out. In fact Um concarned sometimes. Tearke tuther mornin', I cum in fer a cup o' corfee, an' she say: "Cen yer mearke it yerself, Um busy." She'd got the pearpa open at the partners pearge wirra pencil in har hand. I say: "Wot ever are yer a readin' tha' for?"

She say: "Tha's a rummin' wen yer think about it, how many men there are that hent got a partna." I say: "Wus the problem – you hev." She say: "Um lookin' thru 'em just incearse the wheel cum orf. Tha's handy ter hev a nearme or two up yer sleeve."

Har back bin playin' har up agin, she think tha's got suffin' ter do wi' our bed. She say: "I think we orter tearke tha' 'ole faatha bed orf, tha' ent good fer yer back." I say: "You hent cumplearned about it afor, an' tha' hent upset my back." I thort tha' wus lovely an' cumfy, 'specially arter she'd puffed it up. You hatter git a pair o' steps ter git into bed. Enyhow, just ter keep the pearce I said we'd tearke it orf.

We chucked it in the corner o' the bedroom, an' wen the 'ole faathas started ter settle tha' seemed ter spread futher an' futher inta the room like suffin' from outa spearce. In the ind we werra jammin' over it ter git inta bed, an' she say: "I carn't put up wi' this eny longer, we'll hatter see if we can git it in the shud." There's nothin' wass than moving' a faatha bed. In the ind we ended up a rollin' onit.

We got it ter the stairs an' the missus say: "I'll go down an' you cen give the 'ole thing a push." Tha' must a bin gittin' a bit thin, cause by the time tha' got ter the bottom there wus faathas everywhere. But we managed ter git it in the shud.

Wife fer sairle.

The missus a bin inter polotics fer a lot o' years

June, 1994

B' the toime you git this here latter, tha' ole Elaction'll be uva. My missus reckon she's gorn ter wote Tory. I say, "Wot aver for? You allus wote fer one o' them other parties." She say, "I know I do, but tha' Paul Howell a' got such luvla eyes when he cum on the Tele, I fair he's lookin' strairt at me. If I din't wote forrim I fair I'd be a-lettin' onim down." I say, "Tha's the fust toime I iver hard o' anybody a-wotin' fer a blook corse he'er got nice eyes."

O'corse the missus a bin inter polotics fer a lot o' years. She'er bin Poll Clerk fer this willage an' round about. I used ter hairt elactions. They were long ole dairs. I hatter tairke har all ova the shop then gorn git har lairter on.

In the ind I thort, "Enuff is enuff." I hed ter hev it out wirra. "If you tearke tha' on anymore tha's yer lot" I said, or wads ter tha' effect.

Come the next Elaction, she say, "I'm a-gorn ter be Poll Clerk agin." I say, "You know wot I said." She say, "Wotta yer gorn ter do about it?" I say, "You'll see." I hed a good idea. I wrut out a nuttice, "WIFE FER SAIRLE, GOOD CONDITION, WILL EXCHANGE FER YOUNGER MODEL." I putit on the Pearper-shop nuttice-board wirrout the missus a-knowin'. Cum the nexter mornin' she go up the shop. She coont mairke out why evryone wus ser nice ter har till in the ind someone say ter her, "Did you know you're up fer searle?" The man wot kept the pearper shop reckon tha' brought a smile ter people's fairces. After all there ent much ter smile about on Elaction Dairs. If yer look at peoples' fairces as they go ter wote, they look as if the're gorn' ter the dentist, an' wen they cum back they look as if ther'e bin.

As regard ter sellin' the missus, I unly hed one orfer an' tha' wus from a blook who said he'd hev har if I got out. So not unly wus I a-gorn ter git rid o' the missus, I wus a-gorn ter lose my home an' all. I thort tha' ud pay ter leave well alone, arter all she ent a bad ole gal!

"Give him a red card."

Warld Cup tand the missus' life upside down

July, 1994

Tha's rite nice Mr Editor, ter hev you ter rite to, someone ter share ma problems wi'. Tearke the missus, (I wish you would) – an' yit tha' ent ser much har fort as it is foo'ball. This here Warld Cup thing. Har life seem ter be tand upside down. She like foo'ball, we buth on us do, but she seems ter be gorn uva the top this time.

She wook me up tuther mornin'. I say ter har: "Yure a-gittin' up arly arn't yer?" She didn't say nothin'. Tha' tanned out she wus just a-cummin' ter bed. Tha' wus just a-breakin' day – must a bin pushin' fer tree o'clock.

I got up round about seven an' took har a cup o' tea. She just give a grunt. Then I went an' got the pearper, an' mearde sum toost. About nine I thort I batter go an' see if she wus still alive. She wus but she din't look too sharp. B' the time she cum round, tha' wus time fer har ter think about the dinner. Wha' I'm tryin' ter say is, This compatition a just started, wha's she a-gorn ter be like b' the middle o' July? Tha' dorn't bear thinkin' about. We hed a good ole tork ter sort out the problem, but there dorn't seem ter be a way out. She say, "Why dorn't you git a vidio then I cen watch it durin' the day?" Ter me tha' dorn't seem ter be the answer. I like ter do a bit o' writin' in the mornin', I dorn't want foo'ball on then. Cum about dinner time I like ter watch the Test-Match, but she dorn't go nothin' on cricket. As you cen see I can't put my foot down too hard corse I hent got a leg ter stand on.

She cum up wi' the perfect answer. She would listen to it on the wireless. I wus happy wi' tha'. She wus a-gorn ter use one o' them things wot you plug in yer ear. The wireless plug is my side o' the bed. The lead en't long enuff ter go har side, but the plug tha' go in har ear is, so I hed this here wire a-gorn my fearce. Evry time suffin' excitin' happened, she jumped up the bed an' she wus a-sayin' things like, "I hairt corners" or "Give him a red card or send 'im orf."

In the ind we hed ter admit tha' warn't a very good idea arter all. Then she say.

"Why dorn't we chenge sides?" I say, "I're a-bin a-sleepin' this side o' the bed ever since we're bin married, I'm blowed if I'm a-gorn' ter chenge now fer the likes o' Jack Charlton or Andy Townsend. She din't say nothin'. Tha' looks ter me as if she's a-winnin' 1–0 at the moment but I'm hopin' ter force a draw.

She gi' me a Weddin' Aniuwasery Card.

42 year – tha' hent bin too bad

July, 1994

I got orf ter a bad statt us-mornin'. Tha's Tewsdy an' tha's a bewaful day. I took the missus har usual cup o' tea about seven or a little arter, opened har windas, looked out, an' evrything wus luvly.

I thort, "This is the day the Lord a-mearde, let us rejoice an' be glad in it," but tha' feelin' warn't goin' ter last fer long. I say ter the missus, "How are yer this mornin'?" She give a sort o' grunt.

I went inter the back plearce an' read the pearper. The missus cum thro'. She gi' me a kiss, I thort, "Wot the flyin' a got inter har," but I din't say nothin'.

Then she say, "Do you know wot day this is?" I say, "Tewsdy ent it?" She say, "Yis, but wot else?" "Well" I say, "Tha's Stallum Searle day." "Not tha', there's suffin' else. Wus the dearte?" I looked at the pearer. "June 28" I say, "Dorn't tha' ring a bell?" I thort rite hard. I say, "You're lorst me." Then she say, "What happened fotty two year ago terday?" I say, "I'm blowed if I know, a lot o' water a gone under the bridge since then."

"Are you a-tellin' me you realla dorn't know?" she say. Then she cum up wi' the killa punch an' gi' me a Weddin Anniwasery Card. I say, "Is tha' as long ago as tha'?" She say, "Yis, can't you remember tha' day?" I say, "I know one thing, tha' wus bloomin' hot just like tha' is terday. We went ter Clacton fer our honeymune.

"Suffen else I remember, I han't finished buildn' our house an' we went away an' din't hev a front door on but my Dad hung it while we wa gone.

"Apart from tha' I can't recall much else about it. I know the fast pot o' tea you mearde but you din't put a mat under the teapot an' tha' took the warnish orf the tearble, an' the mark is still there today."

She say, "I wus young then. I'd never run a house afore. How many times hev I hard you say, 'The man tha' can't mearke a mistearke carn't mearke nothin'. Why dorn't yer think about the good times we're hed?" I say, "Such as?" She say, "I dorn't know but I're bin happy livin' wi' you this last fotty two year hen't you?" I say, "When you cum ter think about it tha' hent bin too bad – just one! Tha's when she hulled the oven clorth at me. We buth larft.

If I sit down I'm in the way.

A long toime since the house a looked ser clean

August, 1994

Rite now the missus seem ter be mixed up in the hadd warld o' bizness.

Tha's all ter dew wi' har carpet sweeper. The one she're bin a-usin' I dorn't know how menna year is a thing suffen loike a flyin' sorser an' that's still a-doin' a good job, but wen the news learked out tha' she wus still a-usin' a machine tha' old, the Boardroom Boys said, "Enuff's enuff. This woman from Hickling in Norfolk must be pu' in har plearce."

By a majority wote they decided the kindest way ter dew it wirrout a-hartin' har feelins tew much would be ter stop mearkin' tha' type o' dust bag. By dewin' tha' she'd be forced inta a-buyin' a more up ter dearte model.

The reason fer har ole machine a-lastin' ser long is the fact tha' she dorn't use it werry orfen. I arn't goin' ter say the missus is datty. She just wearnt till the floor is covered wi' lolly sticks, sweet pearpers, orange pips, bits o' Lego an' jigsaw an' the odd crisp packet. Then arter a toime wen things git ser bad she'll dew suffin' abou' it. She're bin a-usin' one o' these sweepers wot yer push b'hand but tha' dorn't seem ter dew the searme sort o' job.

Then she cum up wi' the happy thor' tha' if she got a new one tha' ud be a good thing fer the country an' mite even git someone orf the dole.

In the ind, the missus wus a-torkin' ter a friend o' hars. She hed a nearly new one tha' she din't want, so the missus say, "I'll hev it orf on yer." Tha's a much different thing ter har old un, but she seem ter be gitten' the hang on it. Tha's called Henry. There's tree wheels on the bottom on it an' yer pull it ahind on yer as yer go along. She say, "Tha' fear ter be loike tearkin' a dorg fer a walk."

In the few dears she hed it, she're bin trew the house two or tree toimes already. In fact, tha's a long toime since the house a looked ser clean.

So now she's set up. As if buyin' Henry en't enuff, she's gone ter the expense o' buyin' a faather duster. She saw one in our pearpa shop mearde from real faathers.

With all this cleanin', I've got another problem. If I sit down I'm in the way corse she wanta move the chair an' if I stand up I mustn't stand still dew I git flicked wi' the faather duster. This toime o' the year I cen go inter the garden out o' har way. Cum the cold wather I can see moiself forced ter go inter the shud.

How are yew a-gittin on?

I thort I got out o' tha' well

August, 1994

Hev yew ever thort o' tearkin' yar missus ter Somerleartin' an' gor'n in tha' there mearze, tha' is if yew want ter looz har fer half an hour or so. Tha's an idairl plearce ter tearke the children too. We took the grandorters there. They thort tha' wus fun, though the missus statted ter worry wen we coont find 'em. Howsumever they tanned up arter a bit an' we all got out agin'.

Yew dorn' hatter go as far as tha' ter git lorst though. I went raspbry pickin' wi' the missus tuther mornin'. We parked in a gret ole fild then follered the signs ter where the cairns war. As we war a-gorn' we met a women who say ter me, "Tha's a long while ago since we saw each other. Do yew remember we war at schule tergather?" I say, "My hatt tha's gorn' back a bit, dorn't the time fly! Yew're bin suffen busy hen't yer, pickin' all them there raspbries?" She'd got sum mess on 'em. I say, "Would yew like me ter help yew ter carry 'em?" She say, "Yes please", so I told the missus ter go an' mearke a start an' I'd see har in a little while. Enyhow this woman wanted ter chat about ole times an' I wus gone nearly an hour.

I thort I'd batter see if I could find the missus. Well bor, tha' wus a job. Them there raspbries were taller than me an' full o' learf. There wus twe'y one rows an' they looked ter be about a quarter o' mile long. While I wus a-lookin' few har a well spoken man said ter one o' the blooks a-warkin' there, "Excuse me young man, I seem to have lost my wife. Have you seen her?" This blook say, "Learve har nearme in the orffice, if I come acrorse har I'll let yer know, but dorn't worry, we allus lose two or tree a season. We find 'em arter a bit when the leaves drop orf." I dorn't think he thort tha' wus wery funny.

By the time I found the missus she'd got all the raspbries she needed. I say, "Hello my luv how are yet a-gittin' on?" She din't hev too much ter say.

When we got home, I mearde a fuss on 'er 'an helped har ter mearke sum jam. I told har I'd tearke har out cum Saturda nite. She say, "Tha'll be nice." She hed a nap arter dinner an' wen she wuk up she was as rite as rain. I thort I got out o' tha' well.

The Missus got hold o' my arm.

Me an' the missus a bin on a sort o' a holiday

September, 1994

I reckon you've bin a-wondrin' where the flyin' I bin corse I hent writ ter you leartly.

Well I'll tell yer. Me an' the missus a bin on a sort o' a holiday, an' we hent bin out o' Norfolk.

Our mawther Carol a bin away fer a few dairs, so we hed har plearse at Ashill. Tha's a nice willage with a big green, street lights an' pearvements but altho' they're got two nice ponds, they hent got ser much water as wot we hev at Hicklin'.

We hed a mornin' at Hunstanton. Tha' wus suffin' hot. We hen't bin there few uva 20 year, but tha' din't seem ter a-changed a lot. Then the missus say, "How about us gorn ter see the Queen at Sandringham?" I say, "Yis, tha'll be nice." She say, "Do yer think we orter let har know we're a-cummin' corse she might want ter git an extra pint o' milk in ter mearke us a cup o' corfy?" I say, "No, she'll be there, she dorn't go out an' about ser much these days an' she hev lots o' visitors so she's sure ter hev sum."

Anyhow wen we git there, she wus out.

The missus wus everser done, corse she'd tricolearted harself up a rummon. She'd washed har hair the night afore. She din't need har ole' blue coat corse tha' wus a nice day, but she hed har black dress on, an' a string o' parles (not as good as Her Majesty's o' corse) wot she'd picked up at a jumble sale an' har high heeled shoes. In fact I say ter har, "You look smart."

She say, "Do yer think so?" I say, "Yis, do I wunt a said so would I?"

We hed a good ole jam around. My hart tha's a grat house, but she look arter it well. The missus reckon she must hev sum help, she'd never doo all tha' on har own. Then we went round the garden. You never see nothin' like it. My hart there's sum mess o' grass ter cut. We walked from there ter the chach. The missus got hold o' my arm. She say, "I feel touched ter think tha' you an' me are a-walkin' on the searme path as Har Majesty walk on, dorn't tha' do suffen to yer?" I say, "Such as what?" She say, "You know what I mean." We went inter the Chach. Tha' ent wery big but tha's a bewaful plearce. There's a seat there tha' say, "Royal Family Pew" but we warn't allowed ter go an' sit there. When we come away the missus say ter the blook on the gearte, "Do yer mind tellin' the Queen we're bin an' we'll pop in agin when we come this way." He din't say nothin'.

"Givvus a pail o' water Missus"?

That reminds me... of a day of disasters I'd much rather forget

October, 1994

A frend'o the missus come in tuther mornin'. She wus a' tellin' the missus about someone in the village had had a chimly fire.

She say "Cen yer rememba last year wen yer nearly hed a fire here?" The missus say "Dorn't remind me about tha'."

Dorn't let on ter har I told yar, but I'll tell yer wot happened. The dust cart cum of a Tharsdy, an' the tree men cum in fer a cup o' corfee, like they allas do.

While they were a-standin in the back plearce a drinkin' onit, the missus say "I're got a tin o' cinda muck. Cen I gorn hull it in the back o' yar cart?" They say "Cors yer cen." The men hed their corfee an' said "See yer next week."

No sooner hed they gone, wen one o' these blooks cum a-runnin' back, opened the door an' say "Girrus a pairl o' water missus, your're set lite ter our cart." All the missus hed wus an ole plastic pairle wi' sum tearters in. So she shot 'em out in the back yard an' filled it up wi' water.

He ran orf wi' tha' an' the missus filled up har washin' up bowl in cearse they wanted sum more.

Any how, they put it out alrite. The missus say "Wot would a happened if I really hed set lite ter their cart?" I say "I can't bear ter think about it." I say "You'd a hed yer nearm on the front pearge o' the EDP in grat ole' latters, 'Housewife set lite ter dust cart.'"

She say "Alrite, dornt rub it in."

As if tha' wernt anuff fer one day, the missus asked me ter tearke har ter Wearfud ter pick sum onions. I parked the car in a grat ole' field.

The missus say "Are you gorn ter lock up?" I say "Yis." She say "I'll leave my hand bag under the seat." I got out o' the car, the missus locked my door, she got out an' locked hars, an' the keys were still in the car. We were miles from anywhere. I mobbed.

I say, "You gorn pick up yer bloomin' onions, I'll see if I can find a brick ter brearke the glass." Just then, as if an answer ter prare, a blook an' his wife cum ter their car parked next ter mine. I say ter this blook, "Yer dornt happen ter hev a bit o' wire onya, I're locked my keys in the car?" He say "This is yer lucky day, I wark in a garage." In no time atall he got in the car. The missus say "Wot a day, I never woulda got up if I could a told."

I dint know what ter do fust.

Blackberra pan looked like a volcairno eruptin'

October, 1994

The last two or tree weeks as we go out a-walkin' round the village lairns we tearke a chip wirrus an' gather sum blackberras. I should think we're got well uver a stun. Tha's a rum ole job. We git stung wi' nettles, (they allus fare ter grow where the best blackberras are), an' pricked wi' brumbles, but we dorn't mind tha'. We're got used to it arter all these years. I reckon a-pickin' the fruit is the best part on it. The bit I dorn't like is the mearkin' on 'em inter jam or jelly.

The missus a gor a grat old pan fer the job. Har aunt from Russon give it to har fifty year ago so you cen tell tha' a mearde plenty o' jam in its time. She boil all this here fruit up. Then she strairn it uvernite. The next-a-mornin' she add the sugar, then tha' hatter be boiled up agin. I find the best way ter help is ter keep rite out o' har way.

I did statt orf a-helpin'. She say, "Cen you keep on a-stirin' on it a minute an' dorn't let it boil uver or ban on the bottom o' the pan." I say, "You cen leave it in my hands dear, I know wot I'm a-doin'." She say, "I just wanta slip up the shop, I shorn't be gone long."

You're got a good idea wot happened next! I unly left the bloomin' pan fer a minute a two ter go inter the front room, wen I thort I hard suffen. I ran inter the backplearce. Well bor, you never saw such a mess. This syrupy mess wus a-bubblin' an' runnin' uver the top o' the pan an' on ter the hotplearte. Tha' wus a- smokin' away an' tha' looked like a volcairno eruptin'. I din't know wot ter do fust. Knowin' the missus like I do, I thort, "I'm a-gorn ter git suffin' wrong." I took the pan orf the stove. Tha' dripped on the floot an' on ter har best bit o' coconut mattin'. I did hev the sense ter put a bit a' pearper on the tearble afor I put it down. The I looked at the stove. I thort, "Wotever do I do fust?" This stuff wus stuck hard ter evrything. I wondered about gittin' a chisel an' hammer an' chippin' the wust on' it orf, but wus I gorn' ter git it orf afor the missus got back. Afore I hed a chance ter do enything she wus at the door. "Hello my luv" she say. "How's the jelly a-comin' on?" I say, "Wery well, I think tha's done." The she looked round. Well you should a-hard wot she called me. Tha's wen she told me ter git rite out o' har way for at least two hours. She wus nearly all day a-cleanin' up the mess.

Tha' wus a few dears ago now an' eversince then, evrything we eat seem terbe blackberra flearvered. How about you a-tryin' sum blackberra flearvered grilled bearcon. At least tha's suffin' different!

"I bet a ton o' them weigh suffen."

My missus gorn ter put the garden down ter set aside

October, 1994

I should a met Fred at Aircle Sairle last Tharsda. We were a-gorn' ter have a drink tergather. (Sorry Fred I din't see yer, I din't go arter all. We hed the family uver. One wanted ter do this and the other wanted ter do tha' an' in the ind we din't do nothin'.)

I warked wi' Fred years ago an' we're kept in touch ever since. He was a pairnter an' decorairtor, one o' the ole schule, hard warkin' but not uver fussy. He done a job fer a woman from Stalham. She cum inter the yard ter pay har bill. I say ter har: "Are yew pleased wi' the wark done?" She say, "Yis but yar pairnter din't pairnt on top o' the doors." I say: "Fred is in the yard, I'll ask 'im ter cum an' hev a ward wi' yer." This woman say, "Morning' Fred, I're paid my bill but I're just said you din't pairnt on top o' the doors." Fred say: "I'll tell yer suffen else missus, I din't paint the bottom on 'em either."

Well tha's all go about here. The wather is good an' the farmers a gittin' on a-ploughin' an' drillin'. Not unly tha', they're a-gittin' them ole sugar-beet up an' all. Then there's the tearters. My hart dorn't they do well these dairs. My missus wus a-lookin' out o' the winder tuther mornin' wen a grat trairler full o' spuds went past. She say: "I bet a ton o' them weigh suffen'. Hev yew thort how many chips tha' lot ud mearke?" I say: "I should think yew want ter eat more chips, ye're puttin' on too much weight as it is. You orter git out in yar garden an' lose some on it." She say: "That en't fat, tha's muscle." I say: "If tha's muscle, tha's all the more reason for yer ter use it."

She hen't done nothin' ter har garden since the spring. You niver see such a mess. Things a all growin' tergather wi' fat hin an' bineweed. I say: "When are yew gorn' ter do it?" She say, "I thort I'd leave it alone fer a year or so, an' be like the farmers an' put it down ter set aside. I din't say nothin', but between yew an' me Mr Editor, did yer ever hear anybody talk ser much squit?"

"Tha' hit me rite on the hid."

Blood running down ma fearce an' stinkin' like a railway sleeper

November, 1994

I're got a little ole shud up the ind o' my garden where I keep all my tools – spairde, fork, lawn mower an' boxes o' things tha' I want ter keep away from the missus.

Tha' wus nice tuther mornin' so I thort I'd put sum creo on my fences an' rails. Anyhow I found my creosote, tipped sum on it inter a tin, got my brush, an' wus all set ter mearke a statt.

Wen I cum out o' the shud the wind blew the door shut, an' tha' hit me rite on the hid. Not only tha', the tin o' creo fell out o' my hand an' tha' ran all down my trousers, socks an' shoes.

There I wus, blood running down ma fearce, an' stinkin' like a railway sleeper.

I went in an' give the missus a shout. She say, "Dorn't yew cum no futher, look at the mess you're a-mearkin' on my floor. Yew batter go in the shud while I git the dwile an' clean it up. I aren't hevin' yew in here like tha'. Yew batter strip out an' I'll bring yew sum hot water in my washin' up bowl, then yew cen hev a bath learter on." So I went in the shud, (Tha's the one near the back door).

Wen she sum I say, "wot about my hid?" She hed a good look at it. She say, "You'll be orite, praps tha' knock sum sense into yer."

She put the trousers an' socks in the bin, She say, "I aren't gorn ter wash them no more."

I hed a good ole wash, There I stood. I shouted, "Wen are you a-gorn ter cum wi' my clean clothes?" She say, "I'm a-lookin' fer sum old uns fer now." She did bring 'em arter a bit. Then I went an' hed a cup o' corfee ter calm me down, I kept indoors all the rest o' the mornin'.

Arter dinner she say, "Are yew a-gorn ter do your fences this arternoon?" I say, "You must be jokin!"

Wen tha' wus time fer bed, the missus say, "I cen still small tha' ole stuff. Tha's a-mearkin' my eyes water.

"I think tha' ud be a good idea if yew go inter the spare room just fer ternite until the smell die down a bit," so I did just ter please 'er. She say, "Yew cen bring me a cup o' tea in the mornin'. Goodnite." I didn't say nothin!

My hart, the missus fearce went red.

Wot the flyin' is the missus a-doin' in Cromer?

November, 1994

The noites a-pullin' in now an' tha' git learte arly, an' tha's waas since they mucked about wi' the clocks. I dorn't mind corse tha' gi' me a chance ter catch up wi' my readin' an' writin'. One thing about it is tha' keep the missus in an' all. She can't go nowhere on har ole bike corse she hen't go' ner loites on it.

Tha' dorn't rairly mearke no difference ter me if she's there or not corse she dorn't say a lot. She just sit there a-knittin' til' about harf arter nine, then she'll say: "Are yew a-gorn ter mearke the corfee?"

Then arter the ten news she say: "I think I'll go up the wooden hill, are yew a-comin'?" (Tha's an old expression o' hars eversince we lived in a house.) The next I hear from 'er is "Are yew a-gorn ter mearke a cup o' tea?", an' tha's the start o' another day. I mislead yew a bit wen I say she dorn't go out of a noite. She do hev one noite out. Har friend a got a car an' she call fer the missus an' they go orf, so I dorn't say nothin'. If I did she'd only bite my hid orf. All I know is, wen she cum hoom she seem ter be in a good mind an' tha's suffen' ter be thankful for.

We did hev a nice noite out tergather last Saturday. We're go' a few friends a-livin' in Cromer, so we thort we'd go an' wisit 'em. We called on tree on' 'em an' they war all out so we giv up the idea an' walked along the front, then inter Garden Street an' hed a fish an' chip supper.

The missus hed a small harf wi' hars. She said I mustn't hev one on account o' me a-drivin'. She told the gal ter bring me a cup o' tea. I din't think tha' wus wery fair an' I told har so but she just larft.

Enyhow, wen another gal brought the bill, she say ter the missus: "Hello, how are yew a-gettin' on?" the missus say: "Orite, do I knew yew?" She say: "I sarved yew last Tharsdy, you hed a friend along wi' yer."

My hart, the missus fearce went red. I din't say nothin' nor did she, but tha's got me a-thinkin'.

Wot the flyin' is she a-doin' in Cromer of a Tharsdy noite? Yew dorn't go all tha' bloomin' way just ter git fish an' chips, corse yew pass tree o' four fish shops between ours an' Cromer.

If any o' yar staff live round there, praps they'll keep an eye open an' tell me wot she's up to. You can't miss har corse she'll be wearing har blue coat if tha's on the chilly side.

They war a nice green colour.

That key just warn't enywhere ter be seen

December, 1994

Dear-o-dear! Wot a job. I think tha's a good thing we dorn't know wus round the corner, dew we'd never go out o' the gearte.

Tearke tuther nite for instance, tha's the missus forlt as usual. We went an' saw sum friends o' ours at Catfield. Wen we got hum agin the missus say: "Hev you got the key?" I say: "No you locked up, you must a-go' it." She say: "Are yew sure?" I say: "Yis, are yew a-tellin' me yew hen't got it?" There we stood in the putch dark. Wot the flyin' could we do? We got a torch from a nearber, had a good ole look around the yard an' in the car. Tha' just warn't enywhere ter be seen. The missus statted ter git savage. I thort ter maself: "Tha's all I need. Tha's bad anuff losin' the key an' not bein' airble ter git inter the house, but tha's nothin' compared ter har a-gittin' har shat out. In the end we went ter a phone an' arsked our friends if they'd hev a look round ter see if she dropped it as she wus gittin' in the car. They did find it an' brought it over. She soon chenged har tune once she go' indoors, but I thort wot about if I'd lorst the key instead o' har, tha' dorn't bare thinkin' about.

There is sum good news as well tho'. The missus say: "Will yew git me a new pair o' shoes?" She hed a picture o' sum she wanted so I thort I'd git 'em without har a-knowin'. Tha' ud give har a nice surprise. I took this picture ter Yarmouth an' went in a shoe shop. The blook say: "Yis I're got sum like that, I'll go an' git 'em." Wen he told me how much they corst, I say: "I aren't a-payin' all tha' fer them, they wun't be ner good if tha's a bit muddy, she unly want 'em ter go gallivantin' out on a Tharsda night," so I din't git 'em. He gi' me a funny ole look. Arter tha' I drawed on ter the Market. There wus a stall there a-sellin' rubber boots. I thort fer a minute: "Did she hev sum or not? I hen't sin any leartly." So I got har a pair. They war a nice green colour. As they din't corst ser much as them there stupid shoes wud a done, I got har two packets o' linin pegs ter go wirrem. I hen't give 'em to har yit, but wen I do I bet she'll be suffen pleased dorn't yew?

Our room looked like the Castle Mall.

Knowin' har, tha' pay ter tearke a day at a time

December, 1994

The missus a come up wi' a startlin' idea. She say ter me: "Cum the New Year I'll get up fast. Tha's time I started ter look arter yew a bit." I thort: "Wot the flyin' a got inter har? I'll believe tha' wen tha' happen." Knowin' har like I do, tha' pay ter tearke a day at a time. She do seem ter be in a good mind rite now. I think she's a gittin' excited cos we're goin ter be at 'ome fer Christmas an' we hen't done tha' fer tree or faur year. Enyhow she say: "If I'm a-gorn ter git up fast, yew'll hetter git me an alarm clock corse I'll niver wearke up." I say: "I'll git yer one, tha's a cheap price ter pay fer gittin' yer out o' bed of a mornin'."

She're go' har puddins maerde, done just about all har shoppin' an' go' har cards all riddy ter pust. I helped har ter rite on the cards. As we were a-gorn' trew the list we cum acrorse the nearme Cyril. I say: "Who the flyin' is Cyril wen he's up an' dressed?"

She say, "Oh I'll do tha' one." I din't say nothin'.

Then we hed a problem wi' our Chrismas tree lites. Tha' seem ter happen evra year. Wen we git 'em out the bloomin' things unt never go. I must a-spent an hour tryin' ter git em' ter cum on. In the ind I say: "I're hed anough o' this. I'll git a new set." Just as I wus about ter put the new set on, the missus wus a-fiddling' about wi' the old uns an' they lit. I say: "Wud yew now do?" She say: "Nothin'." (Tha' wud be har who go' 'em ter go, she mearke it look as I dorn't know nothin'.) So ter year we're go' two sets o' lites. The missus say: "Tha' mearke our front room look like the Castle Mall."

There's suffen else wot bairt me. I see she're put a bit o' mistletoe above the door goin' inter the back plearce. I say: "Wus tha' for?" She say: "Yew niver know who might tan up. I'm gor'n ter be prepared." I shall hatter finish now corse she's a-shoutin'. She want me ter blow up sum balloons. She reckon she hen't go' ner wind. I say: "Yew must be jokin'." She say: "Wud yew say?" I say, "Nothin' my luv," but I thort all the more.

Best wishes ter yew an' all yar Staff an' ter all them people wot write ter me. Hev a wery Happy Christmas an' a Peaceful New Year.

I wus bloomin' cold.
She say: "Yew mite a-known wot tha' ud be like."

Tha' wus nice a-walkin' terwards Hossey ...

January, 1995

Tha' wus such a nice day a-Sunda the sun wus a-shinin', but the wind wus a bit on the nippy side.

Arter we'd hed our dinner, the missus say: "Wot er yew a-gorn' ter dew this arternoon?" I say: "Watch the futball on the box." She say: "No yew aren't, yer-a-gorn' ter tearke me fer a nice long walk along the beach. Tha'll dew yew more good than a-sittin' there." So we went ter Waxham. Wen we go' there, there warn't another passon in site.

At the high-tide mark there wus a lot o' bits o' wood alayin' so the missus say, "Le's git 'em. We cen tearke 'em hum an' yew cen sor 'em up then we cen put 'em on the fire, tha'll help the coal." So we put 'em in a pile near the gap ter pick up arter we'd hed our walk.

Tha' wus nice a-walkin' terwards Hossey.

We held hans, in fact the missus wus quite ramantic. Wen we tarned round ter cum back tho' tha' wus a diffrent kittle o' fish – tha' wus hid wind an' my hart tha' wus suffen' cold.

The missus wus orite corse she hed har big blue coat on an' har butes, har fluffy hat an' har Norrige City scarf, but I was bloomin' cold. She say: "Sarve yew rite, yew must be sorft cummin' here dressed like tha'. Yew mite a-known wot tha' ud be like."

Wen we go' back ter the gap at Waxham, dear-oh-dear! I cen hardly bear ter tork about it. Someone hed nicked our wood. The missus go' harself in such a stairt I thort instead o' tearkin' har home I'd tearke har fer a ride. Once we go' on the rood she fergo' about the wood.

We went ter Warcut an' set in the motor an' looked out ter sea. She enjoyed tha'.

Wen we warr a-cummin' home we saw a nuttice tha' said: "Herrin'". The missus say: "Shell we git sum?"

This blook tha' wus sellin' on 'em reckon he'd just cort 'em. The missus say: "The're so fresh the're still warm."

Wen we got home she cleaned them there longshores an' say, "We'll hev a pair a piece fer our tea."

She reckon there's only one thing ba'er an a nicc longshore. I say: "Wus tha' my luv?" She say: "Two."

So if yar missus ever feel a bit fed up, git har sum longshores, tha'll cheer har up yew mark my wads.

All I want now is a fishin' rod an I'll be set up.

She Can't Bann the Candle at Buth Ins

January, 1995

Well Christmas is uver fer another year. We hed a luvla time, tho' the missus reckon tha'll be nice ter git back ter normal agin. (Wot iver tha' is.) Tha's all these here learte nites wot do it. I tell har, "Wot yew're go' ter remamber is, yew arn't tharty eny more. Yew carn't keep up ter these young uns." I must say she do the best wi' wot she're go', an' she dorn't look too bad once she git har warpaint on. Even wi' tha', tha' dorn't seem ter do the searme job tha' did a few year ago. She wus in the bathroom asmornin' a-daubin' this stuff on har faerce. I say, "Yew wanna mix sum pollyfilla wi' tha'. Tha's good fer fillin' up cracks." She say, "Dorn't tork such a load o' squit."

Yew know I told yer I go' har a pair o' rubber butes, well I give 'em ter har on har bathday tha' wus just afore Christmas. Har fearce dropped a bit wen she saw they warn't them smart shoes she wanted, but she mearde out she wus pleased wirrum. They wurra bit on the big side so I told har she could hev a pair o' my socks tha'd nearke 'em fit ba''er. She say, "A-wearin' them mearke me fairlike I'm a-gorn' a-fishin. All I want now is a fishin' rod an' I'll be set up." I think she wus a- tryin' ter be funny. I hope so, corse she dorn't know nothin' about fishin'.

Torkin' about learte nites, I nearly fergot ter tell yer. I go' har tha' alarm clock she wanted so she could git up fust. Well tha' hent dun ner good as yit. She say she'll statt wen we're finished a-gorn ter these here parties. She say she can't bann the candle at buth ins.

We went ter sum friends tuther nite. During the evenin' the women went inter the kitchen ter git the grub riddy – so they said! Arter sum time they all cum back inter the room where us blooks were. I looked at the missus. Har fearce wus suffen red. I thort ter muself, "I know wot ye're bin up to" but I din't say nothin'. Tha' wunt a bin rite in front o' all them people. I go' on ter har wen we go' humm. I say ter har, "Why dorn't yew keep ter a small harf instead o' all tha' other stuff?" I think she wus too far gone, tha' went in one ear an' out o' the tuther. No sooner wus har hid on the pillar than she wus away.

I wish yew all the best fer 1995 – if yew dorn't need it I do.

CROMER AND NORTH NORFOLK FESTIVAL
OF MUSIC, DRAMA AND DANCE

Tuesday, 10th May, 1994

Norfolk Dialect Class 2:
17 years and over.

Certificate of Distinction
presented to

MICHAEL BRINDLD

Keith Stiffer
Adjudicator